American
Civil War
Reference Library
Cumulative Index

American Civil War
Reference Library
Cumulative Index

Cumulates Indexes For:

American Civil War: Almanac
American Civil War: Biographies
American Civil War: Primary Sources

Lawrence W. Baker,
Index Coordinator

AN IMPRINT OF THE GALE GROUP

DETROIT · SAN FRANCISCO · LONDON
BOSTON · WOODBRIDGE, CT

Staff

Lawrence W. Baker, *U·X·L Senior Editor*
Carol DeKane Nagel, *U·X·L Managing Editor*
Tom Romig, *U·X·L Publisher*

Rita Wimberley, *Senior Buyer*
Evi Seoud, *Assistant Production Manager*
Dorothy Maki, *Manufacturing Manager*
Mary Beth Trimper, *Production Director*

Michelle DiMercurio, *Art Director*
Cynthia Baldwin, *Product Design Manager*

Marco Di Vita, Graphix Group, *Typesetting*

Library of Congress Cataloging-in-Publication Data

American Civil War reference library cumulative index / Lawrence W. Baker, index coordinator.
   p. cm.
   "Includes indexes for: American Civil War : almanac, American Civil War : biographies, American Civil War : primary sources."
   Summary: Indexes the volumes (Almanac, Biographies, and Primary Sources) in the "American Civil War Reference Library."
   ISBN 0-7876-3819-6 (softcover)
     1. Hillstrom, Kevin, 1963– American Civil War. Almanac—Indexes. 2. Hillstrom, Kevin, 1963– American Civil War. Biographies—Indexes. 3. Hillstrom, Kevin, 1963– American Civil War. Primary sources—Indexes. 4. United States—History—Civil War, 1861–1865—Juvenile literature—Indexes. 5. United States—History—Civil War, 1861–1865—Miscellanea—Juvenile literature—Indexes. 6. United States—History—Civil War, 1861–1865—Biography—Juvenile literature—Indexes. 7. United States—History—Civil War, 1861–1865—Sources—Juvenile literature—Indexes. [1. United States—History—Civil War, 1861–1865—Indexes.] I. Baker, Lawrence W. II. Hillstrom, Kevin, 1963– American Civil War.

E468.H556 1999 Index
973.7—dc21   99-046921

Copyright © 2000
U·X·L, an imprint of The Gale Group
27500 Drake Road
Farmington Hills, MI 48331-3535

Printed in the United States of America

10 9 8 7 6 5 4 3 2

American Civil War Reference Library Cumulative Index

A=American Civil War: Almanac
B=American Civil War: Biographies
PS=American Civil War: Primary Sources

A

Abolitionist movement
  A 4, 15–29, 36, 44, 53;
    opposition to, 20; ties to
    religion, 18
  B 1: 105, 106–7, 116, 174, 213;
    2: 365, 366, 420, 430,
    446–48, 495
  PS 1–2, 30, 36
Abolitionists
  A 15–29, 42, 71
  PS 67, 78, 84
Adams, Charles Francis
  A 94–96, 95 (ill.)
Adams, John
  A 95
Adams, John Quincy
  A 21, 36, 63, 95
African colonization
  A 16–17
Alabama
  A Reconstruction in, 245;
    secession of, 68
Allen, Richard
  A 16

American Academy of Arts and
  Letters
  B 1: 217
American Anti-Slavery Society
  A 21
  B 1: 116; 2: 495
"American Apocalypse"
  PS 31–34
American Colonization Society
  A 16–17
American Eclipse (horse)
  PS 50–51
American Red Cross
  B 1: 1, 9
American Revolution
  A 3, 204
American Slavery as It Is
  A 22–23
  B 2: 496–97
  PS 2
Ames, Adelbert
  B 1: 74
Anaconda Plan
  A 108–9
  B 2: 359–61

1

Calhoun, James M.
  A 192
  PS 124, 125–26
Calhoun, John C.
  A 33, 37, 38–39, 39 (ill.),
    41
  B 1: 42
California
  A 41
  B 1: 146–47, 189
Cameron, Simon
  A 103
Carney, William H.
  B 2: 379, 379 (ill.)
Carter, Jimmy
  A 231
Cass, Lewis
  A 41
Chamberlain, Joshua L.
  A 151
  B 1: 71–80, 71 (ill.)
Chancellorsville, Battle of
  A 145, 148–49
  B 1: 75, 226; *2:* 257–58
  PS 99, 107, 111
Chapin, Graham
  B 1: 152
Chase, Salmon P.
  A 45
  B 1: 46; *2:* 447
Chattanooga, Battle of
  A 140, 160, 162;
    Southern abandonment
    of, 158–59
  B 1: 53–54
Chesnut, James, Jr.
  B 1: 82, 83 (ill.)
Chesnut, Mary Boykin
  A 166; and Southern
    view of war, 101
  B 1: 81–87, 81 (ill.)
Chickamauga, Battle of
  A 140, 160
  B 1: 53; *2:* 456–57
  PS 108
Child, Lydia Maria
  A 17
Civil Rights Act of 1875
  A 242
Civil rights movement
  A 235, 251
  PS 168

Civil War
  PS family conflicts
    caused by, 17–19, 27;
    military leadership in,
    38–39, 41–42
Civil War soldiers
  PS emotions and
    experiences of, 37–48
Civil War songs
  A 186
Clay, Henry
  A 35, 40 (ill.), 40–41, 85
Clayton, Powell
  A 249
Cleveland, Grover
  A 63
Clinton, Bill
  A 246, 246 (ill.)
Cobb, Howell
  B 2: 410
Cold Harbor, Battle of
  A 183–84
Colfax, Schuyler
  PS 156
Colonization
  A 16–17
Committee on
    Reconstruction
  PS 174
Compromise of 1850
  A 28, 41, 42–44, 57
Compromise of 1877
  A 250–51
Confederate Army
  A experiences of soldiers
    in, 146–47; illness and
    disease suffered by
    soldiers in, 182;
    uniforms of, 113–14,
    115; victories in West,
    131–32
  PS military leadership in,
    38–39, 41–42;
    recruitment of soldiers,
    110–11
Confederate cavalry
  PS 49–63
Confederate commerce
    raiders
  A 91
Confederate Congress
  PS 73

Confederate Constitution
  A 72
Confederate guerrillas
  PS 73–79, 81, 83–84
Confederate States of
    America
  A 69–70, 74 (map);
    formation of, 71–73. *See
    also* South
Confiscation Act
  A 208
  PS 34, 65–66
Congressional Medal of
    Honor
  B 1: 71, 78
  PS 96
Conscription Act of 1863
    (North)
  A 156–57
Constitutional Union Party
  A 64–65
Contrabands
  A 208–10
  PS 66
Copperheads
  A 187, 197
  B 2: 481, 483
Cordley, Richard
  PS 78–81
Cotton
  A 6; South's decision to
    withhold from
    European markets,
    90–93
Cotton gin
  A 2, 6
Crane, Stephen
  B 1: 24, 25, 25 (ill.)
Crater, Battle of the
  B 1: 63, 69
Crimean War
  B 1: 5
Crittenden Compromise
  A 70–71
Crittenden, John
  A 70, 72 (ill.)
  PS 27
C.S.S. Virginia
  A 122
Cuba
  A 93
Cumming, Kate
  A 172–73

Cushman, Pauline
  B 1: **89–92**, 89 (ill.), 91 (ill.)
Custer, George Armstrong
  B 2: 330, 386–87, 387 (ill.), 442

D

Daguerre, Louis-Jacques-Mandé
  B 1: 42
Daniel, John M.
  B 2: 342
Davis, Jefferson
  A 73, 79, 87, 104, 106, 109, 124, 129, 174, 175, 238; capture and imprisonment of, 229–30; defiance of, 224, 227; and fight for Chattanooga, 158–59; and flight from Richmond, 224, 227; and Lincoln's reelection, 198; and recruitment of soldiers, 125–26; and relationship with Johnston, 163, 187; and Richmond bread riots, 159; and siege of Vicksburg, 155; and use of black soldiers, 222–23
  B 1: **93–103**, 93 (ill.); and assassination of Abraham Lincoln, 1: 32, and Beauregard, Pierre G. T., 1: 16, 17, 18; and Bragg, Braxton, 1: 51, 52, 54; and "Dixie," 1: 216; and Fort Sumter, 2: 272; and Hood, John Bell, 1: 204, 205–6; and Johnston, Joseph E., 1: 244–45, 246, 247, 248, 249, 250; and Lee, Robert E., 2: 256, 259; and Pollard, Edward A., 2: 339, 342, 344; and spies, 1: 90,

183; and Stephens, Alexander H., 2: 407, 412–13; and Tompkins, Sally L., 2: 463; and Van Lew, Elizabeth, 2: 490–91; and Wirz, Henry, 2: 505
  PS 16, 108, 160; flight from Richmond, 136; and view of war, 122
Davis, Varina
  B 1: 83, 101
Declaration of Independence
  A 8
  PS 104
Delany, Martin R.
  B 1: **105–12**, 105 (ill.)
Delaware
  A 84
Democracy
  PS 104
Democratic Party
  A 48–49, 54, 63–64, 68, 78, 187, 249
  B 1: 110–11
  PS 90, 112, 116, 165, 174
Devil Knows How to Ride, The: The True Story of William Clarke Quantrill and His Confederate Raiders
  PS 79
Dix, Dorothea Lynde
  A 170–71, 171 (ill.)
"Dixie"
  B 1: 216
Doubleday, Abner
  PS 22–23, 23 (ill.)
Douglas, Stephen A.
  A 41, 44, 47–48, 55–59, 57 (ill.), 64, 65–66
  B 2: 265, 269–70, 271, 281, 367, 410, 482
Douglass, Frederick
  A 7, 18, 19, 19 (ill.), 21, 25, 135, 203, 204
  B 1: 57, 107, **113–20**, 113 (ill.); 2: 430, 469, 476
  PS 31–36, 35 (ill.), 88
Dover (Ohio) Historical Society
  PS 77

Dred Scott v. Sandford
  A 52–54, 55, 56, 57, 215
  B 2: 347, 351–52
DuPont, Samuel
  B 2: 403

E

Early, Jubal
  A 150, 188, 189, 193, 194, 196
  B 2: 330, 331, 385–87
Edison, Thomas
  B 1: 46
Edmonds, Emma
  B 1: **121–26**, 121 (ill.), 123 (ill.)
Election of 1864
  B 2: 314–15, 366–67
Electoral college
  A 62–63
Emancipation Proclamation
  A 134–36, 143, 201, 206–7; effect on European neutrality, 97
  B 1: 109, 177; 2: 273–74
  PS 65–72
Emerson, John
  B 2: 348–50
Emigrant Aid Society
  A 46
Emmett, Daniel Decatur
  B 1: 216
England
  A 3; reaction to Trent Affair, 94
Europe
  A neutrality during Civil War, 91–92, 132, 149; reaction to American Civil War, 87–97
Everett, Edward
  PS 105
Ewell, Richard S.
  A 150

F

Fairbanks, Calvin
  A 25

Holsinger, Frank
PS 41–46
Homer, Winslow
B 1: 195–200, 195 (ill.),
199 (ill.)
Homestead Act
B 1: 231
Hood, John Bell
A 160, 187, 191, 199
B 1: 201–9, 201 (ill.),
249; 2: 395, 457–58
PS 122, 131, 134
Hood's Texas Brigade
B 1: 203
Hooker, Joseph
A 143–45, 145 (ill.),
148–49, 162
B 1: 68; 2: 257, 258 (ill.),
320
PS 107
Hospital ships
A 172
Hough, Daniel
A 81
Houston, Sam
A 73
Howard, Oliver O.
A 240, 240 (ill.)
Howe, Julia Ward
B 1: 211–18, 211 (ill.),
215 (ill.)
Howe, Samuel Gridley
B 1: 212, 213

I

Independence, Missouri
PS 76
Industrial Revolution
A 12
International Red Cross
B 1: 8

J

Jackson, Andrew
A 34, 34 (ill.), 63
Jackson, Thomas
"Stonewall"
A and Battle of Antietam,
133, 134; and Battle of

Chancellorsville, 148;
and First Battle of Bull
Run, 114; and Second
Battle of Bull Run, 131;
and Shenandoah
Campaign, 128–29
B 1: 35, 36–37, 150,
219–28, 219 (ill.)
PS death of, 107, 111,
112 (ill.), 114
James, Frank
PS 84
James, Jesse
PS 83 (ill.), 84
Jayhawkers
PS 73
Jefferson, Thomas
A 5, 7, 8–9, 9 (ill.), 34, 35
John Brown's Raid
B 1: 55, 59–60, 61, 213
Johnson, Andrew
A 234, 237–39, 238 (ill.),
240, 242, 243;
impeachment of,
245–48; pardons former
Confederates, 238;
pardons Samuel Mudd,
231; Reconstruction
policies of, 238
B 229–40, 229 (ill.); and
assassination of
Abraham Lincoln, 1:
29; and impeachment,
2: 424–25, 451; and
Nast, Thomas, 2: 336;
and Reconstruction, 1:
192; 2: 414, 422,
450–51; and Seward,
William Henry, 2: 363,
369
PS 151, 153, 160, 161,
162–64, 168
Johnson, Lyndon B.
PS 168
Johnson, William Ransom
PS 50–51
Johnston, Albert S.
A 120, 121
B 1: 16, 17, 51, 164
Johnston, Joseph E.
A 112 (ill.), 155, 178,
179, 224; and campaign
against Sherman, 185,

187; and First Battle of
Bull Run, 112–14; and
Peninsula Campaign,
128, 129; and
relationship with Davis,
163, 187; and
Sherman's March to the
Sea, 221–22
B 1: 16, 54, 183, 205–6,
223, 241–50, 241 (ill.);
2: 256, 312, 394–95,
397
PS 115, 121–22, 134, 146
Johnston, Peter
B 1: 241
Joint Committee on
Reconstruction
A 242
Joint Committee on the
Conduct of the War
A 126
Jones, Absalom
A 16
Jones, John
A 21
Jonesboro, Battle of
A 191
Jordan, Thomas
B 1: 181

K

Kansas
A 45, 47–48, 59
PS 84
Kansas-Nebraska Act
A 44–46, 48, 57
B 1: 58; 2: 269
Kansas State Historical
Society
PS 77
Kate: The Journal of a
Confederate Nurse
A 172
Kearney, Stephen
B 1: 147
Kennedy, Jihmi
A 213 (ill.)
Kennedy, John F.
PS 162
Kentucky
A 84, 85

King, Martin Luther, Jr.
   PS 72
Kirkland, Richard R.
   A 137
Knoxville, Battle of
   B 2: 291 (ill.)
Ku Klux Klan
   A 248–49
   B 1: 135, 142
   PS 175 (ill.), 176

L

Labor unions
   A 204
Lawrence, Kansas
   B 1: 58
   PS 76, 78, 81, 82, 84
"Lawrence Massacre, The"
   PS 78
Lecompton Constitution
   A 47–48, 58, 64
Ledlie, James H.
   B 1: 69
Lee, Robert E.
   A 60, 107 (ill.), 111, 117,
      177, 178, 184 (ill.), 185,
      225 (ill.), 233; and
      Battle of Antietam,
      133–34; and Battle of
      Chancellorsville, 139,
      145, 148–49; and Battle
      of Cold Harbor, 183–84;
      and Battle of
      Fredericksburg, 136,
      138; and Battle of
      Gettysburg, 149–52;
      and Battle of
      Spotsylvania, 181; and
      Battle of the
      Wilderness, 179, 181;
      decision to join
      Confederacy, 107; and
      defense of Richmond,
      179, 218–19, 224; and
      1862 invasion of the
      North, 132–34; and
      1863 invasion of the
      North, 149–52; and
      evacuation of
      Richmond, 224; and
      Peninsula Campaign,

129–30; and Second
      Battle of Bull Run,
      130–31; and siege of
      Petersburg, 218–19,
      223–24; surrender of,
      217, 225–27; takes
      command of Army of
      Northern Virginia, 129;
      and use of black
      soldiers, 222–23; views
      on slavery, 107
   B 1: 167 (ill.); *2:* 251–63,
      251 (ill.); and Battle of
      Antietam, *1:* 45, 66; *2:*
      305, 312–14; and Battle
      of Five Forks, *2:* 381,
      388–89; and Battle of
      Fredericksburg, *1:* 67;
      and Battle of
      Gettysburg, *1:* 76, 77,
      190; *2:* 288–92, 317,
      320–21; and
      Beauregard, Pierre G. T.,
      1: 18; and Brown, John,
      1: 60; and Davis,
      Jefferson, *1:* 100, 101;
      and Grant, Ulysses S., *1:*
      166–68; and Hood,
      John Bell, *1:* 202, 204,
      206; and Jackson,
      Thomas "Stonewall," *1:*
      219, 225; and Johnston,
      Joseph E., *1:* 242, 245;
      and Longstreet, James,
      2: 285, 288, 292; and
      Nast, Thomas, *2:* 337,
      337 (ill.); and Scott,
      Winfield, *2:* 359; and
      Stuart, Jeb, *2:* 435–36,
      438–39, 440–41, 442;
      and surrender at
      Appomattox, *1:* 79; *2:*
      275, 323
   PS 53, 83, 115; and Battle
      of Chancellorsville,
      107; and Battle of
      Gettysburg, 99, 101–2;
      on death of Stuart, 61;
      and deserting soldiers,
      46–47; and siege of
      Petersburg, 136–37;
      surrender of, 138–47,
      143 (ill.), 149, 150

Leigh, Vivien
   PS 132, 132 (ill.)
Leslie, Edward E.
   PS 79
Letcher, John
   A 158
Levin, Carl
   A 231
Lewinsky, Monica
   A 246
Liberator, The
   B 1: 116
Liberia
   A 17
Lincoln, Abraham
   A 29, 55–59, 63, 64, 65,
      65 (ill.), 69, 70, 71, 74,
      80 (ill.), 87, 101, 102,
      103, 106, 107, 112, 125
      (ill.), 145, 185, 229
      (ill.), 234; assassination
      of, 227–29; call for
      seventy-five thousand
      volunteers, 82; and
      creation of West
      Virginia, 110–11; and
      efforts to prevent
      secession of border
      states, 84–85; and 1860
      election, 67–68; and
      1864 election, 177–78,
      187–88, 192, 196–97;
      and Emancipation
      Proclamation, 97,
      134–36, 143, 201; first
      inaugural address, 75;
      at Fort Stevens, 189;
      and Grant, Ulysses S.,
      163; handling of Fort
      Sumter crisis, 77–80;
      handling of Trent
      Affair, 94–96; and
      Northern public
      opinion, 132, 139,
      156–57; political
      leadership of, 157; and
      relationship with
      McClellan, 126–27,
      129, 130, 132–33, 136;
      and Sons of Liberty,
      197; and Thirteenth
      Amendment, 223;

wartime Reconstruction policies of, 237

B 1: 177 (ill.); *2:* **265–78**, 265 (ill.), 271 (ill.), 276 (ill.), 281 (ill.); assassination of, *1:* 27, 29–33; and Battle of Gettysburg, *1:* 76; and black soldiers, *2:* 403; and Brady, Mathew, *1:* 43–44; and Burnside, Ambrose, *1:* 65, 66, 67; and Davis, Jefferson, *1:* 93, 97, 98; and Delany, Martin R., *1:* 110; and "Dixie," *1:* 216; and Douglass, Frederick, *1:* 117–18; and Emancipation Proclamation, *1:* 109; and Fort Sumter, *1:* 14–15; and Frémont, John C., *1:* 143, 149–50; and Grant, Ulysses S., *1:* 165–66; and Greeley, Horace, *1:* 175–78; and Jackson, Thomas "Stonewall," *1:* 224; and Johnson, Andrew, *1:* 233–34; and Lincoln, Mary Todd, *2:* 280–83; and Lowe, Thaddeus, *2:* 299; and McClellan, George B., *2:* 305, 308–9, 312 (ill.), 314–15; and Nast, Thomas, *2:* 335; and prison camps, *2:* 502–3; and Seward, William Henry, *2:* 363, 366–68; and Sherman, William T., *2:* 396; and slavery issue, *1:* 82; and Stevens, Thaddeus, *2:* 421; and Sumner, Charles, *2:* 449; and Truth, Sojourner, *2:* 470, 470 (ill.); and Vallandigham, Clement L., *2:* 481, 482–85

PS 16, 25, 99, 108, 162, 168; assassination of, 147, 152–54, 155,
156–60, 162; and Battle of Gettysburg, 100; and black soldiers, 92–95, 166; and Confederate prisoners, 91; and 1864 election, 112, 116–18, 135; and Emancipation Proclamation, 65–72, 67 (ill.); and Gettysburg Address, 101 (ill.), 103–5; and military draft, 20; reaction to capture of Atlanta, 122; Reconstruction policies of, 150–51, 154; and support from Union soldiers, 118; and visit to Richmond, 137; war policies of, 29, 30, 34

Lincoln-Douglas debates
A 56–58
B 2: 269–71

Lincoln, Mary Todd
A 227, 229 (ill.)
B 2: 268, **279–84**, 279 (ill.)
PS 27, 105, 150, 157, 161

Lincoln, Robert
B 2: 283
PS 157

Lincoln, Thomas (Tad)
B 2: 281 (ill.)
PS 105

Logan, John A.
B 2: 423 (ill.)

Longstreet, James
A 148 (ill.); and Battle of Chancellorsville, 145, 148–49; and Battle of Gettysburg, 150, 152; and Second Battle of Bull Run, 131
B 2: **285–93**, 285 (ill.), 301

Louisiana
A Reconstruction in, 250; secession of, 68

Louisiana Purchase
A 35
B 1: 145

Lovejoy, Elijah P.
A 21
Lowe, Thaddeus
B 2: **295–303**, 295 (ill.), 298 (ill.)

M

Maddox, George M.
PS 84

Magruder, John B.
A 127

Maine
A 35

Manassas, First Battle of. *See* Bull Run, First Battle of

March to the Sea
B 1: 18, 207; 2: 396–97

Martin, Isabella
B 1: 86

Mary Chesnut's Civil War
B 1: 87

Marye's Heights, Battle of. *See* Fredericksburg, Battle of

Maryland
A establishment of martial law in, 84–85; suspension of writ of habeus corpus in, 84–85

Mason, James Murray
A 93, 93 (ill.), 94, 96

Matthews, Robert
B 2: 469

Mayo, Joseph C.
A 159

McCabe, Charles Caldwell
B 1: 216

McClellan, Ellen
B 2: 306, 307 (ill.)

McClellan, George B.
A 111, 116, 125 (ill.), 131, 188 (ill.); administrative and training skills, 118, 120; and Battle of Antietam, 133–34; cautious style of, 126–27; and 1864 election, 177–78, 187–88, 196–97; and loss of command, 136; and Peninsula Campaign, 127–28, 129–30; and relationship with

Lincoln, 126–27, 129,
130, 132–33, 136
B *2:* **305–15**, 305 (ill.),
307 (ill.), 312 (ill.); and
Battle of Antietam, *1:*
45, 65, 66; and Homer,
Winslow, *1:* 197–98;
and Howe, Julia Ward,
1: 214; and Lincoln,
Abraham, *2:* 274; and
Lowe, Thaddeus, *2:* 300;
and Meade, George G.,
2: 319; and Peninsula
Campaign, *1:* 189, 245;
and Scott, Winfield, *2:*
359, 361; and Seven
Days' Battles, *2:* 256
PS and 1864 election,
116–18
McClernand, John
A 106
McCullough, Henry E.
PS 82
McCullough, Hugh
PS 156
McDowell, Irvin
A 112–14, 116
B *1:* 12, 15, 16 (ill.), 183,
244
PS 24 (ill.), 25, 26
McKinley, William
PS 162
McLean, Wilmer
A 226
Meade, George G.
A 149–52, 150 (ill.), 178,
179
B *1:* 76, 190; *2:* 258–59,
289–91, **317–23**, 317
(ill.), 322 (ill.), 441
PS 41, 42 (ill.), 44, 99
Medical treatment for
wounded soldiers
B *2:* 462–64
Mexican War
A 36–37
Mexico
A 89
Miller, Stephen Decatur
B *1:* 81

Mississippi
A Reconstruction in, 249;
rejoins the Union, 245;
secession of, 68
Mississippi Plan
A 249
Mississippi River
A 153 (map), 154–55
Missouri
A 35, 84, 85
PS 74, 81, 82
Missouri Compromise of
1820
A 17, 35–36, 37, 44, 45;
United States after, 18
(map)
Mitchell, Margaret
PS 132
Mobile Bay, Battle of
A 189–90, 192
B *1:* 132–34
PS 116
Montgomery, James
A 211
Morgan, John Hunt
B *1:* 68
PS 53
Morse, Samuel F. B.
B *1:* 42
Mosby, John Singleton
B *2:* **325–32**, 325 (ill.),
331 (ill.), 385
PS 74–75, 75 (ill.)
Mosby's Rangers
PS 74–75, 79
Mott, Lucretia Coffin
A 21
Mudd, Richard
A 231
Mudd, Samuel A.
A 230–31
B *1:* 31–32
PS 160
Mudd, Sarah Frances
A 231
Murfreesboro, Battle of. *See*
Stones River, Battle of

N

Napoléon III
A 88, 89, 90 (ill.), 91

Narrative of the Life of
Frederick Douglass
B *1:* 116
Nashville, Battle of
B *1:* 208; *2:* 457–58
Nast, Thomas
B *2:* **333–38**, 333 (ill.)
Nationalism
PS 104
Nebraska
A 45
Negro Soldier Law
A 215
Neutrality, European
announcements of
A 91–92
New Orleans, Battle of
A 122–24
B *1:* 129–31
New York draft riots
A 157
New York Tribune
B *1:* 171, 172
Newsom, Ella King
B *2:* 464
Nicollet, Joseph Nicolas
B *1:* 145
Nightingale, Florence
A 169, 170
B *1:* 5, 5 (ill.)
North
A celebrations of victory
in, 217, 227;
industrialization in,
103; military leadership
of, 104–8; military
strategy of, 108–9;
naval blockade of
South, 109, 122–23,
188–90; naval forces of,
102; opinion of Lincoln
in, 132, 139; prejudice
against blacks in, 157;
reaction to Lincoln's
death in, 228–29;
recruitment of soldiers
in, 100–101, 102, 103,
116, 156–57;
transportation systems
of, 104; view of war in,
99–101, 115–16, 139,
149, 152, 156–57, 162,

177, 185, 192, 196–97.
See also Union Army
PS attitudes toward
slavery, 1–3, 34; beliefs
about South, 15–16, 20;
manufacturing capacity
of, 49; prejudice against
blacks, 29, 31–32; pre-
war confidence of, 15,
19, 20, 24; view of war,
108–9, 116. *See also*
Union Army
North Carolina
   A secession of, 70, 83
North Star, The
   B 1: 117
Northwest Territory
   A 5
Nurses
   A 169–71, 172
Nursing
   B 1: 4–8; *2:* 463–64

O

"Occurrence at Owl Creek
   Bridge, An"
   B 1: 24
Ordinance of Nullification
   A 33

P

Paine, Lewis
   B 1: 32; *2:* 368, 368 (ill.)
   PS 151
Palmerston, Lord
   A 94
Panic of 1857
   A 55
Parker, Theodore
   A 43
Patterson, Edmund DeWitt
   PS 109–15
Patterson, Robert
   A 112, 114
   B 1: 183
Patton, George
   PS 133 (ill.), 134

Payne, Lewis. *See* Paine,
   Lewis
Pemberton, John C.
   A 154, 155, 156
   B 1: 246
Peninsula Campaign
   B 1: 189, 197, 245; *2:*
   309, 312
Penn, William
   A 4
Pennsylvania State
   Monument
   PS 100 (ill.)
Perryville, Battle of
   A 140
Petersburg, Virginia
   A fall of, 217; siege of,
   218–19
   B 1: 167
   PS siege of, 115
Pettigrew, James
   A 151–52
Phillips, Wendell
   A 18
Photography
   B 1: 41, 42, 43
Pickens, Francis
   A 79
Pickett, George
   A 151–52, 224
   B 2: 287, 290–91
Pickett's Charge
   A 151–52, 151 (map)
Pierce, Franklin
   A 73
   B 1: 95, 97 (ill.)
Pierson, Elijah
   B 2: 469
Pinkerton, Allan
   B 2: 310–11, 311 (ill.),
   312 (ill.)
Pioneer Days in Kansas
   PS 79
Planter (ship)
   B 401–4, 402 (ill.)
Pleasants, Henry
   B 1: 69
Poe, Edgar Allan
   B 1: 42
Poinsett, Joel Roberts
   B 1: 144
Polk, Leonidas
   B 1: 99

Pollard, Edward A.
   B 2: **339–45**
Pope, John
   A 128 (ill.), 130, 131
Popular sovereignty
   A 45, 47–48, 54, 55, 56,
   64
Porter, David
   B 1: 127
Porter, Horace
   PS 138, 140–46
Powell, John Wesley
   B 1: 242
"Prayer of Twenty Millions"
   B 1: 176
Prigg v. Pennsylvania
   A 27
Prisoner exchanges
   PS 91
Prisoners of war
   B 2: 501–6, 503 (ill.)
Prisons
   B 2: 500–506, 503 (ill.)
Prosser, Gabriel
   A 10

Q

Quakers
   A 3, 4, 16
Quantrill, William Clarke
   PS 75, 76–78, 79, 81, 82,
   83
Quantrill's Raiders
   PS 79, 80–81, 82–83,
   84–85

R

Race relations following the
   Civil War
   A 236
Race riots
   A 204–5, 243
Radical Republicans
   A 242, 247
Rangers
   PS 73
Rathbone, Henry R.
   PS 150, 152, 161

siege of Atlanta, 187, 190–91, 192; and total warfare, 193–94, 196

B *2:* 391–98, 391 (ill.); and Forrest, Nathan Bedford, *1:* 135, 140; and Grant, Ulysses S., *1:* 166; and Hood, John Bell, *1:* 205, 206; and Johnston, Joseph E., *1:* 247–49, 250; and "March to the Sea," *1:* 18; and Thomas, George Henry, *2:* 457

PS 18, 60, 115 (ill.), 117, 125 (ill.), 146; and capture of Atlanta, 115, 121–34; and the cavalry, 52; and "March to the Sea," 131, 133, 135; and "total warfare," 121, 123–34

Shiloh, Battle of

A 120–21, 124

B *1:* 16–17, 51, 138, 164

Sickles, Daniel

A 106

Sir Henry (horse)

PS 50–51

Slave rebellions

A 10, 19, 59, 61, 202, 205, 207

B *1:* 59, 61

PS 68, 70

Slave trade

B *1:* 137

Slavecatchers

A 42

Slavery

A 1–14, 51, 56, 89, 97, 207; abolition of, in other countries, 22–23; as cause of the Civil War, 203; compromises on the issue of, 31–49; efforts to abolish, in the United States, 15, 29, 235; expansion into new states and territories, 31–32, 35–36, 37–41, 44–46, 71; growth of, 6, 202; laws limiting, 5; laws

supporting, 2, 27–28; and the Southern economy, 2, 3, 6, 11–12

B *See* Brown, John; Douglass, Frederick; Greeley, Horace; Scott, Dred; Smalls, Robert; Truth, Sojourner; Tubman, Harriet; Weld, Theodore Dwight

PS 15, 65, abolition of, 70; black families in, 2–3; and economy of the South, 1; importance to Southern war effort, 34; Northern views of, 1–3; Southern views of, 31

Slaves

A role in Confederacy during Civil War, 205–6; runaway, 25–28, 42; treatment of, 7–10, 12–13

Slidell, John

A 92 (ill.), 93, 94, 96

Smalls, Robert

B *2:* 399–406, 399 (ill.)

Smith, Edmund Kirby

PS 82

Smith, Frank

PS 85

Smith, James

PS 155

Society of Friends. *See* Quakers

Songs of the Civil War

A 186

Sons of Liberty

A 197

B *2:* 485

South

A and Conscription Act, 124–26; considers using black soldiers, 222–23; economy of, 218, 222; efforts to win support of Europe, 89–93; industrialization in, 103; military leadership of, 104–8; military strategy of, 109–10; naval forces of, 103–4;

opinion of North in, 110; racism toward blacks in, 222–23; recruitment of soldiers in, 100–101, 102, 103–4, 124–26, 152; shortages in, 158–59; and states' rights, 125–26; supplies of, 194–95; transportation systems of, 104; view of Lee in, 129–30; view of war in, 99–101, 115–16, 156, 160, 198, 217–18, 220. *See also* Confederate Army

PS beliefs about North, 15–16, 20; economy of, 1, 108; manufacturing capacity of, 49; pre-war confidence of, 15, 19, 20, 24; reaction to Stonewall Jackson's death, 114; treatment of slaves, 35; view of war, 108–9, 133. *See also* Confederate Army

South Carolina

A 33–34, 66, 69, 76; Reconstruction in, 244, 250; secession of, 68

Southern states

A rejoin the Union, 245

Spies and spying

A 173–75

B *1:* 35, 92, 123, 182, 183, 184; *2:* 489–91

Spotsylvania, Battle of

A 181

Springfield, Illinois

PS 159

Stanton, Edwin M.

A 103, 122, 130, 247

B *1:* 111 (ill.); *2:* 308

PS 156, 162

Stanton, Elizabeth Cady

A 21

States' rights

A 32–34, 37, 38, 54, 58, 125–26

B *1:* 95

PS 15, 30–31